Ulysses Elijah - My Story

From Thief to Wheel Chair Racer

How a fall from six stories saved my life

As told to, edited and transcribed by Henry Intili

Ulysses

My name is Ulysses Elijah. I was a thief, a drug addict, a drunk and a womanizer. Now I am a nationally ranked wheelchair racer.

I want to share my story with you. As you read my story, I hope and pray that you, your family, friends, and partners will find it a blessing to your hearts and minds.

Let me begin my odyssey with a description of the town of Waynesboro in Burke County, Georgia where I was born and raised. You probably never heard of my town. It's south of Augusta, near the border with South Carolina. When I was growing up, the town had no busses or cabs, no public transportation. A freight train rumbled and clanked through the center of town several times a day– a train with no passengers. You wanted to go someplace, you walked, drove a car or tractor, rode a bicycle or a horse or a mule. Mostly we walked.

I didn't know my father as I was growing up. He was never around for us. My mom tried to raise my three brothers and a sister. But she got sick in 1957 and was sent to a hospital where she remained for twenty years. I never knew what her illness was, certainly we children weren't told anything about that.

My auntie, mom's oldest sister, and her husband took in my brothers, sister and me. She already had six children of her own, so she had to raise eleven kids. This made life very hard for all of us. We were living in a small house in a poor South Georgia town with hardly any money for anything. A dollar was a big deal.

That small house was called a board house – the walls and floors were plank boards. Wind whistled through the walls. You could see the ground below through the cracks in the floor. The house was built on piers, there was no foundation. I hated going under that house for anything. I was scared of the snakes and spiders and anything else that might be under there.

In the 1950s life was flat hard for Black folks living in rural Georgia. No one had much money or much of anything. The house had no inside water or bathroom for us – we had to use an outhouse. It certainly had no air conditioning or even a window fan to move the hot, humid air of Georgia in the summer. And no central heat to warm the cold winter wind blowing through the walls and floor.

Auntie and uncle did what work they could as uneducated black folk. They plowed with mules in the spring, broke corn and weeded fields in the summer, picked cotton in the fall. That was a hard life. You ever try working in the hot Georgia sun all day long to make a few dollars? The weather bad, you stayed home and made no money. No health insurance, no sick day pay.

Many times as a young boy, in the middle of the night, I would urinate on myself rather than go outside into the dark night. Me and my brothers slept together in one bed. That meant the brother closest to me had to sleep in my urine too. That caused many angry fights with punches and yelling.

I thank God that Auntie took us in, and we didn't have to go to a place where we would be separated. Later, on down the line, we were separated.

This was a rough time for me. We four brothers had to do most of the work around the house – tote the wood, cut the wood, bring it into the house, and build fires in the fireplace for warmth and in the kitchen wood stove for cooking. We carried buckets of water into the house from a hand-pump well in the back yard, swept the dirt yard, and did all kinds of stuff like that. We took the hard part.

When my sister and two older brothers left Auntie's house, that left me without a father or an older male figure in my life. They left town and came back now and then but didn't visit or stay regular.

We were real poor. When Christmas came around, I didn't get any toys. I didn't get the big red wagon I always wanted. Auntie's oldest son was the same age as me – he got the red wagon.

Auntie took us in – I thank God for that. But she always treated her children better than she treated us. Many times I had to get up in the morning, fetch water from the well, and go to school with no clean clothes. When I came home, I couldn't watch television or cartoons the way her kids could. I had to tote the water and cut the wood.

Of course, I didn't do well in school. No one at home told me to read every day, to study or do my homework. School wasn't important to Auntie and Uncle. They probably didn't have much schooling themselves. That's a sad thing. The schools were segregated, of course. If you graduated from the black school, there wasn't much chance of doing anything like college. Most of the courses were designed to train you for some kind of physical labor or maybe the basics of a trade. Nothing that would help you outside Waynesboro.

The truth is my reading skills now are at the third or fourth grade level. I believe that if my school years had been better, maybe my life would have been better, maybe today I would have a regular job and a regular family. Of course, in that case, you wouldn't be reading my book, and I wouldn't be the man I am.

Today I encourage my grandchildren and every adult I meet to keep working at your reading and writing skills. Keep pressing in there! Don't give up! If you keep trying, God will help you.

In the seventh grade, when I was fourteen, I dropped out of school. I wasn't listening to the teachers, I was being disobedient. There was nothing there for me in that school. I went to work in the fields. I picked cotton and drove tractor like most of the black men in that part of Georgia. What else was there for us to do?

That's when I started drinking. My older cousins and I hung out drinking. I was drunk a lot. I remember the last time I came home to Auntie's house drunk. She told me I had to leave.

The first two times I came home late at night drunk, she beat the hell out of me with a stick. She whopped me good. You had welts when she laid into you. The third time, I came home to a woman as cold as a January morning.

"This is my house," she said. "And you need to get out." She had a stick in her hand. As drunk as I was, I knew there was no point in arguing with her or trying to answer her back.

My oldest cousin was already married. I packed my few clothes and went to live with him. Certainly, I didn't think about going back to school. My farm work gave me the money to party, drink beer, smoke reefer, and hang out on the street. That's what I most remember about being fifteen and sixteen.

When I was seventeen I met this girl named Maydoris. We hung out together and went to dating. That led to our first child Topeka. After our second child Cassandra, we got married.

Being married with two young children didn't stop me from drinking and sneaking around on my wife with other girls. Pretty soon I had another child by one of these girls.

My wife and I had two more daughters. One of them – Towana – died. Then I had Johnny and Ulysses, Jr. So, in all I had six children, five by my wife Maydoris.

None of this stopped me from drinking, smoking and hanging out with my friends. Sometimes I would be gone for days or weeks. Lots of times I stayed with another girl. When I got back home, I fussed at the wife and kids. If gives me no pride to admit that I beat on my kids, but I never beat my wife.

Money was always a problem. I made good money where I worked. Most of the time, Maydoris would go to my white boss and pick up my check. That way she knew that she and the kids would have money.

I got my drinking money from stealing.

I started burglarizing trailers to steal food and anything else I could find. One Saturday night I was in a trailer, I opened a door in the back of the trailer. The owner was standing there with a hand gun. I slammed the door in his face, ran through the trailer and out the front door as fast as I could. I ran through a nearby soybean field in the dark, moonless night. The man was shooting at me. God helped me that night – the man's aim wasn't as good as his anger, and I wasn't killed or maimed.

There was a Mennonite mission near us. They let us into their home for meals. I repaid their kindness by stealing the church money. When they were out of town, I went into their house and stole food.

In one house I was robbing, I found a pistol and a shot gun. I stole those and sold them. Those folks knew it was me stealing from them. They could have had me locked up, but they didn't. They could have pressed charges against me, and I would have been convicted.

The missionary folks cared about me and tried to reform me. They even came by my house and took me to church with them. For years I worked for them.

There was a club in town where I drank and picked up women. Lots of time, late at night, I broke into the club and stole cold beer, liquor, cigarettes, and anything else I could find.

These people I was stealing from, I knew them very well. They knew I was doing the thievery. But no one caught me. My wife knew what I was doing; my family knew what I was doing. Nobody could talk to me, nobody could stop me.

I was mean and violent. And I was not listening to anyone tell me anything. This bad behavior of mine went on for years. Thank God I was never really hurt or killed doing these bad things in Waynesboro.

A few times I was sent to jail for a month or two. My family and friends would get me out. The same people I abused and stole from!

In the mid-70s, when I was 26, I moved to Atlanta. My mom had left the hospital and moved to Atlanta. That gave me the chance to leave Waynesboro, my wife and children and my problems with them.

I was working at a dairy in Waynesboro then. Even though I was still living with my wife, I had a girlfriend. I was abusive to my wife and abusive to my girlfriend too. She got tired of messing with me and all the problems with that. She went to JobCorps, they found her work in Atlanta. She told me she was through with how I was treating her, and she left.

I remember the a Sunday morning right after she left. I was sitting on the porch after my milking job, looking out at the field across from my house, thinking of her, thinking what a mess my life was with my wife, and how I hated being here.

I packed a small suitcase with my clothes, got in my car, and drove to my Auntie's house. In the rear view mirror I saw my wife running down the road after me, crying and yelling to me. I paid no attention to her and drove on.

At Auntie's house, I met my cousin, sold my car to him for a little money and asked him to drive me to the Greyhound station. I caught the bus for Atlanta and never gave Waynesboro or my family a single thought on the whole bus ride. I told myself I was glad to be free.

In Atlanta, my mom was pleased to see me, but we really didn't know each other, we were strangers. I didn't stay with her long. In those years I lived with her sometimes and I moved in with women friends sometimes. I never had a place of my own.

Atlanta presented me with the opportunities I missed in Waynesboro – a good job, a way to get a high school diploma or maybe even go to college, the opportunity to join the army or the navy or the marines, a chance to buy a nice house. But I didn't think of none of that.

My sister was in Atlanta and she was so glad to see me. She took me down to a place called Mrs. Winters Chicken and got me a job there, so I had some money coming in.

Atlanta and I agreed with each other. My mind was on making money, drinking at clubs, and chasing the pretty girls. When you come from a place like Waynesboro, Atlanta with all those lovely women with their fine hair and their beautiful legs - that could just drive a man crazy. I knew I was living in the best place in the world.

One time I was living with three girls. Well, maybe I shouldn't talk about that.

Looking back, my relationships were always complicated. For example, I met a girl named Debbie. I was real sweet on her. She was living with her grandmother when I first met her, and she had an apartment across the street from her mother. Her brother and his friends lived in that apartment sometimes. After we got together, she moved from in one place to the other and I followed her.

After Mrs. Winters, I started making good money working for a construction company. I was bringing home $400 to $500 every week which was really good money. God had opened a door for me. I started work for them cleaning up messes and gradually, as they trusted me, I moved up to where I was running the heavy equipment – like I did on the farm.

And I walked away from God's open door. The money went for drinking and drugs and a good time. I didn't save a thin dime.

One Sunday afternoon I went to visit this friend who lived around the corner from Debbie and me. He and I often took pills together. I never knew what we were taking. This one time I bought a pill from him. I never asked him what it was, he just told me I would like it. After thirty minutes my mind was completely messed up. I went back home and Debbie got so mad because I was acting crazy and talking weird.

She went back to his place and asked him: "What did you give Ulysses? He's acting wild."

He told her what it was and what to do to stop it. Debbie's sister and her kids went to the store and bought a gallon of milk. She stood over me and made me drink the whole thing. It took two hours for me to calm down.

Another time I was living with this lady. A real nice lady who, like me, had no good foundation. She had two male friends who sold drugs.

One fella sold reefer and the other sold cocaine. She had an office in the back of her apartment. When the reefer man came over, he would go back to the office and bag it for sale. When the cocaine man came over, he set up a cooking operation in that office to prepare the drugs. I used the reefer to get high regularly, but only took an occasional snort of cocaine, not enough to get hooked bad. Now and then we mixed the cocaine with the reefer and smoked that. There are many kinds of ways to smoke cocaine and I tried them all.

From 1983 to 1990 I lived the life of the streets, doing the drugs, stealing purses from old ladies, robbing houses. This is in addition to the money I was making at my regular job.

I believe that my problem in life at that time was I had no foundation. There was no foundation in what was right and what was wrong. I had no skills in how to lead a good life: church is someplace you went because someone drove you there on a Sunday morning. Rules and laws were things to be avoided. Women existed for the pleasure of men.

God put plenty of opportunities to do the right things in my path, plenty of people who wanted to help me. I wasn't paying attention. For example, the time I was with Debbie, who was so good to me, I believe I sneaked around with six or seven other women. Like sneaking in one back door and coming out the other.

During my first years in Atlanta, I turned my back on my family. My sons needed a father like I never had. My daughters needed a father in the house. I never took the time to return to Waynesboro even for a visit. I knew they needed me, I blamed my rudderless life on my lack of a foundation, and I did nothing to give them what I knew I lacked.

In ten years, I had not been back to my family for a visit more than twice. And when I did go back, I hardly spent any time with my sons. I cannot tell you the reason for this – was I embarrassed? Did I lack any sense of responsibility? A dark cloud covers my understanding of my actions in those years. My responsibilities in Waynesboro faded away from me when I was caught up in my fast living Atlanta life.

Sons and daughters need fathers and mothers. I know this, you know this. Yet I failed to do what I knew was the right thing. I pray that one day I will have a good relationship with my children. But I know it won't be because I was a good father to them.

Please don't misunderstand me, back then I loved my life in Atlanta. I lived for worldly things – the pretty women, parties every weekend, the liquor, smoking cigarettes and reefer. I was making good money in those years, some weeks $500. I did not have a checking account, didn't even know what one looked like. The cash went in one pocket and out the other. Paid on Friday, broke by Monday morning. Thirty years old, working for good money for seven years, and not a penny in the bank.

I worked construction and lawn work. High quality work that paid me good money. Many times on a landscaping job at a rich folks house, while the boss was out front trimming a hedge, I would sneak in the back of the house and steal liquor and money. Sometimes I would sit in their kitchen and eat their food out of the refrigerator. One time I even found and stole a gun from a man's house. This was the same kind of stuff I did in Waynesboro. I hadn't learned a thing.

I made nothing out of my life in those years, still not trying to accomplish anything, still not trying to go back to school and get a good education, still not trying to establish myself for the future, still not trying to prepare for retirement, still not trying to prepare for being in my 60s or 70s, still not preparing to be a father or even a grandfather one day, still not being a blessing to anyone around me.

God had given me all kinds of opportunity to get it right. And I didn't hear anything. Still not going to church, still not surrounding myself with strong believers, still not being with people with positive directions, still not being with people who had strong foundations. All I did with God's many chances was to act stupid.

Several times in Atlanta I ended up in jail for thievery and beating up on a girlfriend. My street friends or my girlfriend would get me out.

My family never bailed me out. They were disappointed in me and didn't want to support what I was doing.

Let me tell you how low my life was in Atlanta. One afternoon I was hanging out near where my mother lived. In a parking lot near her place I saw a man and a woman talking. They appeared to be a little tipsy. Not doing anything strange or wrong. I looked left and right, no one else was around. I took a running start and at full speed grabbed that woman's purse and kept running. They screamed and yelled, but I was gone in a flash.

Behind some bushes, I emptied the woman's purse. The only thing in that purse was a thin dime. No cash, no credit cards, just that one dime. I dug through that purse like a squirrel digging for an acorn. That dime was the only thing I found. I threw that purse away with disgust.

I could have been killed if the man had a gun, I could have been arrested if they had caught me. All that trouble for ten cents.

Another time I was near Martin Luther King train station, just hanging out. An elderly woman passed by with grocery bags. I followed her to her apartment building. She put the bags down on the steps along with her purse to open the door. When she stepped in, I ran up to the door and snatched her purse. Fast as I could, I ran away. Her purse had a lot of cash in it. And I did not feel any guilt about stealing her money.

As bad as the things I was doing, I believe that someone was praying for me and God was watching me in my messes. I could have been seriously hurt or even killed doing what I was doing. Even when you're acting up, even when you're doing wrong, even when you're in the wrong place, God is still looking out for you.

Coming into New Year's Eve 1990, I had no money, no job, nothing to drink and no place to go. I thought about this high-rise apartment I used to burglarize a couple times a week. The same one where my mom lived. I went in the back of the high-rise about 10pm. I climbed up from one exterior patio to the next all the way to the sixth floor pulling up from one railing to the next. My body was in wonderful strength. In the darkness, I was as agile and hidden as an alley cat.

The sliding door to the sixth floor apartment was unlocked and I entered the apartment. A man was laying down on his bed sound asleep. On his dresser I found his billfold and took the money from it. I went into the living room and looked around. There was nothing there for me to steal.

Back in his bedroom, I must have made a sound because he suddenly woke up. He stared at me and I stared at him. He didn't come at me with a baseball bat or a knife or anything like that. We just kept staring at each other. Finally I walked out the back door on to the patio and went to climb on the railing.

I looked calm, but inside I was boiling with fear and anxiety. Climbing from one outside terrace to another isn't anything like you see in the movies. You have to be real careful, you have to concentrate real hard where you put your hands and your feet. You can't let your mind wander. And seeing that man's eyes in the bed – that broke my concentration.

Suddenly, the worst thing happened to me. Somehow I lost my balance and fell six stories. Six stories! I remember hitting tree limbs as I fell through the air. I landed on the sidewalk with a terrible crash that pounded through my whole body. I lay there for a minute before I tried to get up. I knew I was hurt, hurt real bad.

I couldn't get up. My legs wouldn't work. I tried over and over to raise myself up to get out of there. I had to get out of there before that man in the bed got up and called the police. The best I could do was to drag myself forward with my hands. My fingers dug into the dirt and grass. In front of me I found a stick that I threw against a window on the first floor.

A man finally came out of that apartment to see who was making noise. He saw that I was lying on the ground.

I said to him: "Sir, my name is Ulysses Elijah. My mom lives on the seventh floor. Could you or someone please get my mom and tell her I'm hurt and can't get up?"

I guess he thought someone was playing a trick on him because he went back into his apartment and didn't help me. I lay back on the ground for another thirty or forty minutes feeling scared and sorry for myself. I kept telling my legs to get up and work. But they didn't. Every time I tried to get up and failed, I got more and more scared. Why won't my legs work when I need them!

I pulled myself along with my hands and elbows, my legs dragging behind until I found another stick, or maybe it was a cane. I threw it at this man's first floor apartment again. He came out the back door and saw that I was still on the ground.

"Sir, could you please go up on the seventh floor and get my mom, Miss Elijah, and tell her to get me some help. I cannot get up."

This time he must have figured something was wrong because thirty minutes later the police and an ambulance came and found me. A crowd formed around me.

A big African-American man in a dirty shirt that was hung out of his pants said to the police: "This be the man what has been robbing us and stealing our money."

The ambulance people asked me a few questions. I can't remember exactly what they said to me. They put me on a stretcher and strapped me down. Then I blacked out. When I woke up again, I was at the hospital emergency room, lying on another stretcher in a hallway looking up at a bright light. I tried to get off that stretcher, but my legs still weren't working.

They took me for an MRI and wheeled me into immediate surgery. My lower pelvis was smashed. They used pieces from my femur to reconstruct the pelvis.

PART TWO

Have you ever noticed how many things a baby and a young child has to learn in only a few years? How to crawl, how to walk, how to put on clothes, how to use the bathroom. These are things regular people do every day. Things your body knows how to do without thinking. Do you think every time you take pull up your pants? Do you have a mental checklist every time you go to the bathroom?

Now image yourself without the use of anything below your waist. In fact, don't just image it. Try it. Let your legs go completely limp and try to pull up a pair of pants. Borrow a wheelchair, try to open a bathroom door, maneuver in the bathroom, pull down your clothes, move from the wheelchair to the toilet, do your business, clean yourself and then reverse the process.

Let me tell you true: If you want to understand my story in the full after my fall, try that simple exercise. And that's just one small piece of what I had to learn as if I were a baby again.

After my surgery, I started the long process of physical therapy. Maybe I was lucky or maybe God hadn't given up on me because I had a wonderful nurse and physical therapist named Laura Johnson. Laura had been trained at Shepherd Spinal Center and transferred to Grady. The word *tough* doesn't even start to describe Laura. She certainly had to be tough to work with a hard-headed young man like me. Laura was the first of many people who transformed my life. She was, and still is, a dear friend and mentor.

LAURA'S STORY

My name is Laura Johnson. I'm a physical therapist, have been my whole adult life. In all my time as a PT, there is one person who stands out above everyone else for sheer determination and motivation: Ulysses Elijah.

In 1990 I had been a PT with Shepherd Spinal Center in Atlanta for a number of years. My specialty was spinal rehabilitation. In January, work at the Center was slow, and I was posted to a three month temporary assignment at Grady Memorial Hospital in their spinal center.

Several weeks into my assignment, Ulysses showed up. There was an instant bond between us, like a divine intervention. We met, shook hands and clicked. You could see the fire in his eyes.

So many patients come to me depressed, willing to do only the minimum to relearn their bodies, endlessly complaining about their pain and the unfairness of their new disability. Not Ulysses. He was so motivated that in three weeks he accomplished the work of eight weeks. He never complained, he never argued. He pushed me as much as I pushed him.

Paraplegics have an overwhelming experience of loss. You live with the memory of running and walking with family. You live under a constant sword of self-pity and depression. In many ways it's an identity crisis. Your whole life changes; the way people look at you and talk to you changes. People see the chair, not the person.

Let me tell you what a new paraplegic has to do. First, you have to learn where your body is in space. In a person with full neurologic capacity, the legs give balance for sitting as well as standing. Dead legs don't counter-balance the rest of the body when you're seated. You have to learn to use your head and arms to provide the balance normally supplied by the legs. This can be a difficult and frustrating task.

There were times when Ulysses looked at me and said: *You got to be kidding.* Then he noticed my steely gaze, realized I wasn't fooling, and bent into the task with everything he had. Let me tell you – there is nothing in my professional life that feels better than watching a person with full motivation dig in and try hard to conquer his disability.

Ulysses had a mantra – *Make my body stronger.*

At the end of my three month assignment with Grady, I resigned from Shepherd and stayed full time at Grady. Ulysses showed me that Grady was the place where I could help the most. Plus, if I left Grady, I would leave Ulysses, and I believed God had given me his care.

After months of working with Ulysses, an opportunity opened for me in Russia. This was at the time when Shepherd gave me the contacts for wheelchair racing. I asked my friend Nancy to meet and work with this wonderful man. When I returned from my travels, I once again stepped into Ulysses' world. He does that to you.

There is no question in my heart: As much as I helped Ulysses, he helped me.

ULYSSES STORY (CONTINUED):

At Grady they taught me how to take a bath, how to put my clothes on, how to get out of the house if there's a fire – teaching me everything

I needed to know so that I could be independent, so that I didn't have to depend on family and friends to help me do everything.

The folks in my family were in a position to let me live with them. The problem wasn't them, the problem was the physical layout of where they lived. It's time for you to do another experiment. Get back in that wheelchair and try to go from your driveway into your house. Are there any steps? How do you get up them? If you have a storm door and a house door, how do you open them both and wheel inside? Then wheel around the house and try to enter rooms and turn corners. In today's world, we say that a place is *wheelchair accessible*. Don't take my word for it – try it yourself and learn how few homes, restaurants, stores, county offices, state offices, federal offices are *wheelchair accessible*.

Even places that claim to be handicap accessible may not be. Recently, I was in an orthopedic clinic in Atlanta. The spring on the bathroom door was so strong, that someone on crutches could never have opened it. In a wheelchair, with all my upper body strength, even I had a problem.

My mom, sisters and brothers lived in places that had steps to the front door. How does someone in a wheelchair get up a flight of steps?

When I was first released from the hospital I had to stay at a facility in Cascade that was designed to be accessible. But it wasn't the facility itself that caused my first problem.

I couldn't read good. I already told you that schooling was not important to me or my family when I was growing up in Waynesboro. Maybe it's hard for young folks today to know how things were like growing up in segregated rural Southern town. Let me be kind and say that a young black boy who didn't care much for learning wasn't encouraged. If he dropped out of school, that was one less black kid who had to be supported in school with county taxes.

There was always work to do in the fields that didn't require reading or mathematic skills, and plenty of farmers who needed uneducated and physically strong workers. Slavery may have been abolished, but the work the slaves did was still there.

When I entered the home in Cascade, my brother warned me: "Don't let anybody read your mail. Maybe there's things in it they can steal." Now that left me with a real problem. I couldn't make out the words in most of my mail, but I didn't want anyone else knowing my business.

So when the owner of the facility wanted to help me and read my mail to me, I wouldn't let her. She saw a stack of letters into my room and asked me what's in these letters. I told her I didn't know because I couldn't understand them. And I told her that I promised my brother I wouldn't let anyone else read my mail. We got into a pretty heated argument. Maybe she didn't call me stupid, but looking back, that's what I sure was. What good is a piece of official mail if you don't know what it says?

Then I made a big mistake, a stupid move because I was angry at the owner of the facility. I called that old girlfriend who had the friends selling drugs out of her house. She and I had dated for about seven years. I thought she would help me. She and her current boyfriend came and got me and brought me back to their place. "Why, sure, Ulysses," she said. "We want you to come and stay with us. Get you out of this awful place."

I wish I could say she took me in for kindness. I wasn't thinking very straight, wasn't thinking through my anger, or I would have asked why should there be kindness when I treated her bad when we were together?

She didn't take me with her for love or kindness; she took me in for revenge. I stayed in the downstairs of the house and slept on a couch. She didn't feed me regular. Her three daughters thought I was a play toy and pestered me and threw things at me. I soiled myself a lot.

Most days my old girlfriend came downstairs in the morning, ignored me, got her girls off to school and went back upstairs. She wouldn't come back down until late in the afternoon before the girls returned from school.

I cussed and screamed at her. It didn't do no good, didn't impress her or make any difference. Many days the father of the girls would come over. The two of them ignored me and pretended I wasn't there.

I don't know what would have happened to me if her sister and mom didn't help me. To this day I thank her sister for her kindness.

This bad situation lasted for two or three months.

One day my brother and sister-in-law from Florida came by to see how I was doing. He looked around and grew real angry. I was on the couch soiled. He couldn't understand what I was doing in that house with the old girlfriend who hated me. He gave me some money – he didn't have much - and we talked about moving in with my other brother and his family in Atlanta.

What did I do with that money? I was so depressed, as soon as he left, when he was driving down the street, I spent it on drugs and alcohol. When I sobered up, God showed me a door. This time I opened the door and moved in with my brother and his family.

I lived with my brother, his wife and two lovely children. I agreed to pay him rent to let me stay with him. It was a good place for me.

About a month later I was in Atlanta when I met an old friend named Buddy. That was the same day that I had my government check for about $400. We went to his place. Buddy pulled me upstairs in my wheelchair to his room. Then with my money, he left and bought drugs. We smoked cocaine and marijuana all night long until we went through that money.

At six in the morning, when the sun slanted in the window, we were grubbing around the floor trying to find remnants of the drugs. I was out of the wheelchair crawling on the floor. I ended up in the corner of this filthy room, filth all over me.

In that moment I knew this, this filth, this crawling on the floor of a place I never knew, this was my life.

A voice spoke into my heart and said: *You can't do this anymore and live. Get up and go to rehab.* Don't ask me how or why, because I can't answer you, but for the first time I listened to the voice.

Somehow I cleaned myself up and got back into my wheelchair. I told Buddy to get me downstairs. There was a drug rehab center down the street that I had passed many times. I entered the place and spoke to the woman at the front desk. "I need help." I don't recall that I had ever before in my life said those three words. I signed myself in.

I stayed in that rehab for several months, going to meetings, learning more about how to use my wheelchair. One night, I found a small bed sore on my right hip. Because I didn't have any feeling in the lower part of my body, I didn't know it was there.

The rehab didn't know how to tend a bed sore. For several months they put a bandage on it. That didn't do no good. It only got worse. You could see right down to the hip bone.

They placed me with a nice family in Atlanta. Two days later that open sore became infected.

They next thing I knew, I woke with a team of doctors and nurses around me. Someone asked me: *Do you know where you are?*

I told him *I think I'm in a hospital, but I don't know how I got here.* I was confused. It took me a while to understand that I was back in Grady after a seizure. Maybe it was from the infection or maybe it was those drugs I took months back. Whatever the case, I descended into Hell.

Ugly, vicious, snarling demons and evil spirits were crawling up the walls. They were attacking me in all kinds of ways, attacking my mind, attacking my body, attacking me during the day, attacking me in my sleep. They were in my head screaming at me. And I was screaming back. I saw myself in the bed trying to defend myself, but I couldn't. The nurses tied my feet to the bed to stop me from crawling out of the bed and landing on the floor. Later, they had to tie my hands to the bed to keep me from ripping out the tubes that gave me antibiotics for my infection.

My sister on my mother's side came to visit me many mornings after her night shift. I recall one morning I grabbed her hand so tight it took several nurses to pry her free. I didn't want her to go. I wanted someone to stand by me and protect me from the demons.

My sister belonged to a church. She asked a lady pastor and a group of church ladies to visit me in the hospital every day. They prayed for me at the bedside, and they prayed for me in their church. I told them about my life in crime. I told them how my life had gone from bad to worse. I told them about my bed sore that wasn't getting any better. The doctors couldn't do a skin graft because the infection was so bad.

Pastor Millner - God rest her soul, she's gone on to glory - she told me about their anointing oil. They gave me a bottle of this special oil. She told me: *Every time you or the nurse puts a new dressing on that sore, you put some of this oil around it too.*

I did what she told me. A couple weeks later, God had healed that bed sore enough where the doctor could do a skin graft to cover the sore. Between that oil and the skin graft, the sore finally healed over.

But it still oozed pus. They had to cut the leg open from the hip to the knee to clean out the infection. They put a drain in my leg that lasted for a month until the infection resolved.

During this time the pastor and the ladies came to my room and prayed with me. They prayed for me to stay away from drugs, to stay away from cigarettes, and all the other bad things I had been doing with my life.

For the first time I felt improvement. God opened another door for me. This time I looked in. I got stronger and stronger day by day as Pastor Millner and the ladies prayed with me.

After many months, when I was still in the hospital, they told me I was ready to start physical therapy. That's where I caught up with Laura again so she could help me with physical therapy. This time, in addition to working on my body, she started working on my mind, telling me about sports that I could be involved in – basketball, tennis, racing wheel chairs.

What did she see in me that led her to believe I was ready to listen? That I was ready to be something more than a broken down black man with almost no education spending his life sitting around in a wheelchair.

She had a vision of me in a racing chair. And she acted on that vision. One day I went in to physical therapy and she was there with a man in a wheel chair like mine. There next to them was a racing chair. They smiled. "Try it, Ulysses."

Oh, I fit into that chair like a hand in a glove, like a pecan in its shell. It was right. It was me. I rolled around that hospital in the racing chair. You would have thought I was A. J. Foyt racing around Daytona.

When the hospital released me, I went back to live with my ex-girlfriend in Decatur. But this time I was clean. I had the help of the church, I had the help of Laura, and I had a vision for myself.

One morning I took the MARTA train into downtown Atlanta. I decided to find an apartment for myself. I was ready to live on my own.

At the Atlanta Housing Authority a lady helped me fill out the mass of paperwork. When we were done with that chore, she asked me and two other men to come with her to look at apartments. But before we could leave, a plain-clothes detective came up to me.

"Mr. Elijah?"

"Yes, that's me."

"I need you to go with me."

In the wheelchair, he and another detective took me downtown to Fulton County Jail. They booked me and put me in a cell in the hospital section of the jail. That way I could take my medicine and be treated for my wounds that weren't fully healed. I was there for two weeks before I went to court for the crime in the high rise apartment.

In the courtroom with me was my sister who had helped me so much in the hospital and a court appointed lawyer. The white lady prosecutor didn't care that I was paralyzed, or that I was in a wheelchair, or that I would never walk again from the fall that happened during the crime. All she wanted was for me to do time for my crime. She pressed the judge: "He needs to do some serious time. I mean serious time. He stole, he robbed, and he needs to pay for what he's done."

Thanks be to God, the judge looked at me with mercy. Then he looked at that mean white lady prosecutor and said to her: "Look at this man. How can he harm anyone? What more can we do to him? He's in a wheelchair for the rest of his life. I'm going to set him free." The sound of that gavel was the best sound I ever heard.

God opened another door for me. The biggest door he had ever opened for me. Let me tell you what I mean. One day I was taking the number 18 bus into town. I stopped at a grocery store and bought a pack of Kool cigarettes. At the bus stop I lit up that cigarette and God took the taste right out of my mouth. I threw down that cigarette and never looked at another one again.

My life had changed. I continued to go to church, continued to go to the doctor and to my physical therapy, continued to keep myself focused on the goal of racing. All these people were encouraging me to move forward. One nurse at Grady said to me: "Ulysses, we only see you for regular check-ups. You aren't like other wheelchair patients who come back again and again with the same problems. You're special and you're doing great."

Laura and Nancy worked hard with me. They bought me a bike with their own money. They weren't rich and I had no way to repay them except to stay focused. They took me to the race track and I had a vision of heaven.

I felt this strength in the wheelchair. All those years I disappointed friends, I disappointed family, years I fell short of myself, of anything good or positive. Now, here I was with my hands on the racing wheelchair's rubber wheels. And I knew I was going to change my life around, knew I wasn't ever going back, knew I was going to walk a straight road the way I should have from the beginning. I was going through that door God had opened.

There's a man I need to talk about named John. He was a friend of Laura's and a very strong Christian who believed in Jesus. He worked in his office in Roswell. Every week in the afternoon he came in his pickup truck to Decatur to get me and my racing chair. In those days I was eager to start racing in the Peachtree. John told me: "Ulysses, you aren't ready for the Peachtree Road Race. I'm going to make you ready."

First, he showed me where his office was on Alpharetta Street in Roswell. Then he drove ten miles further out into the country. In the early 1990s, there wasn't much development in Forsythe County past

Alpharetta. As we drove up Highway 9, I didn't see any black faces either.

He stopped the truck and took the wheelchair out of the back. I swung myself from the passenger seat into the chair.

"Ulysses, it's four o'clock. I close the office and go home at five thirty. You better be back to the office by then, because otherwise, I'll be gone." Then he got into his truck and left me.

There I was on the side of the road in a wheelchair watching the taillights of my ride fading into the distance up and over a hill. I had no money, and I didn't know where I was. What I did know was Forsythe County was no place for a black man after sundown.

I put my hands onto the wheels and dug in. Let me tell you, taking a wheel chair up hills is a world different from a flat track. And there were cars and trucks whizzing by me. Big trucks with pine tree logs. Big pickup trucks with guns in the back window. I want to say this about that White area – I was never mistreated. No one yelled at me or cursed me.

You've heard of pushing people off a dock into deep water to teach them how to swim? That was me only worse. I pumped those wheels until my arms ached. I had to be back before he left his office.

Week after week John took me farther and farther out into the country to force me to work those arms and get ready for the hills of the Peachtree and the pressure of the race. Mostly it was ten miles from his office. I always made it back to his office on time, and I always knew he meant it when he said I had to be.

In the early 1990s, when you were in the Peachtree Road Race, if you didn't finish the course in a certain length of time, you were pulled off the course. That's what John was training me for – to make sure that I could finish the race within that time frame. Win or lose, he wanted me to finish.

John has been with the Lord for ten or twelve years now. I can still hear him tell me: "Ulysses, whatever you do, whatever happens, don't never, ever quit in a race. If you quit, you're a loser. When you stay in the race, even if you finish last, you're a winner. Don't never quit in anything. Anything."

When I see him again in Glory one day, I will thank him.

Those roads north of Atlanta are not flat, they are full of hills. I had to push that wheelchair hard in the hot, steaming sun. IN our last sessions John gave me 45 minutes to wheel those ten miles. Thanks be to God that God gave me the strength to push the chair hard enough to get back to John's office before he went home for the day.

And, yes, when I finally got to the office, sweaty and exhausted, he was there with a smile. We loaded my wheelchair in the truck, and he drove me back to Atlanta. He did not charge me a dime for his gas, his time or his help.

I'm so grateful for John, I'm so grateful for Laura, I'm so grateful for the ladies of that church, I'm so grateful for Nancy – They encouraged me to move forward. God opened the door, I walked through, and they were there to guide me and move me forward.

MY FIRST RACE

Let me set the scene. The Atlanta Peachtree Road Race is for regular runners or walkers and for disabled racers in wheelchairs. This is a 10K race that takes place on the morning of July 4th. The wheelchair racers go first, followed by the runners. When you're in a wheelchair you have to complete the 10K in less than 45 minutes or they pull you off the course because behind you are 50,000 runners.

Because of John's pushing me and encouraging me, in 1994 I qualified for the Peachtree Road Race. I had to race 10K through those North Georgia mountains in 45 minutes to qualify.

Laura and Nancy (who I will introduce you to later) hooked me up with the Shepherd Spinal Center wheelchair team. Laura got me my first racing wheelchair – a purple beauty. I rolled around the fourth floor of Shepherd several days a week! Now, I thought after all my wheeling through the mountains of north Georgia that I was good. Well, let me tell you, them men on that wheelchair team, they were real good.

I was the only Afro-American on that Shepherd team. They embraced me, they encouraged me, they challenged me, and they never looked down on me in no kind of way. Now almost twenty years later, some of that team have gone on to Glory, some I still talk to, and some are still close to me.

The night before my first Peachtree, I hardly slept. Nancy picked me up at my apartment and drove me downtown so that I could be at the starting line by 6 am. I was registered in the Open Men's Division (ages 20-40). The wheelchair racers had four divisions in 1994: Open Men, Open Women, Masters (over 40), and Quadriplegics.

The Open Men Division had about 80 racers. The past winners were in the front row. I was placed in the back line on this warm and sunny morning. Here I was – never did any sports before my injury, and I was about to race in the biggest sporting event in Atlanta!

Before they dropped the flag, John's words rang in my head: "Whatever you do, don't ever quit during a race."

I was nervous and scared. I was shaking with worry that I was going to finish last or they would pull me off the course because I was too slow.

I didn't win, I wasn't even close to some of these fellas. And I wasn't last. My time was 34 minutes – a good time. I was happy. That time was good enough to qualify me for any future Peachtree Race.

In those days we finished the race in Piedmont Park. The last section had some dangerous curves in the park. Several folks have crashed and turned over on those curves. That's all changed now.

It's time for me to introduce you to someone else: Nancy. She was a blessing to me, a source of endless encouragement. And she says I was a blessing to her. After she worked all day at her regular job at Grady, she would pick me up and take me to the track. We strapped the racing bike to the back of her little car, loadrd our bags into the back seat, and we got gone. She even drove me all over the country to races. Sometimes twice a month we travelled down the highways.

Many days, we didn't leave Atlanta until late in the afternoon after her shift. We didn't get to our racing destination until midnight. Myrtle Beach, South Carolina was one place that comes to mind. That meant we didn't get to bed until one o'clock in the morning and we had to be at the race by seven. This went on for fifteen years and she never charged me a dime. Even now we sometimes get together and drive to a race.

Only one time did we have a bad experience. We were in Myrtle Beach doing a race in the pouring rain. Late in the afternoon, when the races were finished, and people were packing up their tents, the rain stopped. Soaking wet, I wheeled to the car while Nancy walked beside me. The car had a flat tire. While we stared at that tire, unsure what to do, a lady approached us and let us use her phone to call Sears down the road. They told us to bring the tire, and they would fix it.

Somehow we got that tire off Nancy's car, rolled it down the street to the Sears Automotive store, and they repaired the flat. That must have been quite a sight: A black man in his racing clothes and wheelchair along with a white lady rolling a tire. Strom Thurmond probably rolled over in his grave.

During my training for the 1994 Peachtree, I was clean from drugs and alcohol. I continued to go to church and stay clean. But things were not easy for me. I still had trouble reading. My poor education was holding me down.

Before my accident, as I told you, I had no real relationship with my sons and daughters. I was living the "good" life in Atlanta, and they were no more than a distant memory to me. After my accident, while I was in the hospital when the church ladies folded me into them, one night I spoke to the Lord.

"Lord, I need a relationship with my sons and daughters. I have neglected them." God heard me and worked that out for me. I started talking to my older daughter on the phone. At first she was real angry with me, upset and cussing. She told me I had never been a father to her.

I'm sorry to say that many times I had to hang up on her. I couldn't handle her anger even though I knew she was right. I was a bad father to her. But right or wrong, I wasn't going to listen to her disrespect. I was trying to reach out to them. That lasted for several years until we worked things out enough to talk to each other in a limited way.

On Christmas morning in 1997 I was sitting on my bed in my apartment. I asked God to show me everything I had done wrong to people. God wasted no time. He quickly brought my ex-wife to my mind. I took a deep breath and phoned her. "I apologize for abusing you, for walking away from you and the kids, for not being a good husband, for all the wrong things I done to hurt you and to hurt our kids."

She never answered me. To this day, I don't know if she forgave me. I turn that problem over to the Lord. I know someday I will be judged for what I did to her and the kids. And I know that I apologized and asked for forgiveness as God wanted me to. That is a comfort to me.

Today I try the best I can to be a help to my children and grandchildren. My financial resources are extremely limited, but I visit and talk as often as I can. I always encourage my sons and daughters to respect their mother and love her in every way.

God put people in my way to help me. And I wish I could help my children and grandchildren in the same way.

GOODWILL

In 1994 I started in the Goodwill Industries program. They help folks who are disabled in some way. In my case, they had a special program for folks with spinal injuries. My first counselor was Tom Taylor. He was a great support to me, steering me to the right people and job programs in Goodwill. He even came out to my races to watch and cheer for me.

Like everyone else, I started in the Training Program. There were all kinds of people in the program: men and women with speech problems, others were blind, some couldn't use their hands, some disabled through accidents, others born with problems. The Goodwill goal was for us to better ourselves, to teach how to look for a job, how to go on an interview, how to dress, how to speak and listen.

Thank God for Goodwill.

It doesn't sound like much but my first job at the Goodwill training program was to sort shoes. They had so many shoes! I didn't know there were that many shoes in Georgia. A fella named Joe who was disabled with problems walking and I sorted the good shoes from the bad shoes for eight hours a day. That lasted for six months and I'm sure I did a good job. I enjoyed getting up every day, dressing and going to my job. We worked hard, joked and laughed though our eight hours of work. Goodwill paid us for this work and that gave me some extra money.

I remember the first time I got my pictures into the Goodwill paper and their brochures. There were eight of us in the one picture. What is most remarkable is how every one of us is smiling. A real smile because we were really glad to be with Goodwill.

More than anything else, the six month Goodwill training taught me how to be a great employee. More than how to dress and interview. How to greet customers and be happy in my work. Years later Goodwill often had me come back and talk to the new trainees. That was a privilege and an honor.

At the end of my training I thought I wanted to be a clerk or answer phones at a company. That wasn't realistic because my reading and writing skills were so poor. How can you take notes and write things down if you have to take time with every word? Or stumble over what people are saying to you over the phone?

A month after my training program God opened another door for me when Goodwill got me a job at the Marriott Marquis Hotel in

Atlanta. Goodwill had a number of disabled employees at the Marriott. In fact they had an office downstairs on the service level to support their employees. I worked as a lobby attendant where I made sure that lobby was clean, that the brass was clean and shiny, made sure that the bathrooms were clean. I also helped guests with any questions or showed them where the restaurants and shops were located.

I worked at the Marriott for seven years on the Restaurant Lobby Level. Many of the regular guests became friendly with me. And I really felt part of the Marriott employee family. Guests would ask me about my story and my racing. They talked to me about family members in wheelchairs, asked me how that family member could become more involved with life. The Lobby Level was a great place to work.

I remember one lady guest who was in my area several times a week. We said a few words to each other. She wouldn't look me in the eye when she spoke. She had long hair that covered her forehead. She always carried her Bible. One day she admitted to me that she had a scar over her left eye and she was ashamed. She believed that she didn't look pretty.

"You don't got to be ashamed of that scar," I said. "God ain't concerned about that scar. Look at all the scars that Jesus had. He wasn't ashamed of his scars. His followers weren't ashamed of his scars."

She lifted up her head and smiled. That was the first time I ever saw her smile.

I believe God led me to Goodwill and put me at the Marriott to encourage people to lead a good life with the Lord.

I met another lady guest from New York. She was staying at the hotel for four days to get away from her problems. She had been with a man for almost ten years. "I don't know what to do. He hasn't asked me to marry him and I want to be married. The other night I was at the bar. I know I had too much to drink. I started talking to a man there. One thing led to another and we ended up in my room, in bed, having sex. I am so disappointed in myself. What a mistake! I made things worse for myself."

Here she is talking to the king of mistakes in the middle of the hotel lobby with guests and other folks doing their things all around us. "We all make mistakes in life," I told her. "And we're going to continue to make mistakes until we go home to meet the Lord. The problem is when you make mistakes over and over and don't learn from it. Sometimes we allow the flesh to take over. Stuff gets put in our pathway and we trip over that. I got messed up with drugs and stealing. My church helped me and encouraged me."

I was not ashamed to tell this lady about my story and the mistakes I made in life that brought me to the loss of use of my legs or to my life in the wheelchair. There is never shame in telling the truth. A lie never dies. One lie always leads to another.

Me and this lovely young lady talked for almost an hour about mistakes and God's love. God kept my manager away, kept the hotel lobby supervisor away, so that no one interrupted our conversation. I spoke comfort to this lady and God's love to this lady. What good would come from judging her or beating up on her? Why should I tell this hurt lady that she did wrong or she's going to Hell for her actions?

The lady cried. Water poured out of her eyes as we talked. Still no one came around and interrupted our conversation. God protected us. She parted from me with a smile and a thank you.

Another guest I met at the hotel told me that her son was in a wheel chair. "He sits around the house all day and does nothing."

That didn't cut no slack with me. "There's so much we can do in a wheel chair. We have opportunities like everybody else. Just because we're in a wheel chair, that don't mean we can't go out and work or be involved in activities or sports." I told her there are folks who race, who play tennis, basketball, and all kinds of other sports. If healthy bodies can do this, we can too.

"Sometimes families want to keep us in that chair doing nothing because they want to feel sorry for us. Families need to encourage us. When I first came to Atlanta, I was doing pretty good. Then I got caught up in fast living, drinking partying, chasing the women, drinking and drugs. My brothers and sisters were disappointed in me. That fast living and thievery almost cost my life. Then God put wonderful folks in my path and I chose to let them help me. My sister gave me heat and told me to straighten up my life." I hope I helped that lady and encouraged her.

The one thing that bothered me was to see people in one of those powered wheel chairs, folks with the use of their upper bodies who do nothing more than push a button. That only makes us weaker. I know families think they are doing the disabled person a favor with those power chairs, but that's not true. Folks with full upper body function need to use the strength God gave them.

The wheel chair is like a car. You got to take care of it, care of the tires and the brakes and the cushions. And your upper body is like the motor. You got to eat right and take care of your body so you can power that chair. The more you power that chair, the stronger you become. The stronger you become, the more you can do with yourself.

Marriott's General Manager and my direct managers supported me and my racing. They gave me days off so I could travel; they contributed money to help me enter races and pay for my equipment. The managers constantly asked me when was my next race, what was I eating to keep my strength up, did I have enough money for equipment and travel.

Marriott embraced the Goodwill program. There were two wonderful Goodwill staff in the hotel who I need to mention: Stephanie and Quinton. They were the best support anyone could ask for.

I was proud to dress in my black pants, white shirt and bowtie. Many mornings I had to get up at 5am to catch the 6am special MARTA bus that took me downtown to the Hotel so I could be at work at 7am. After six years many of those people on the bus became friends and supporters.

I don't believe any guests or employees had a bad experience with this man in a wheel chair. I never received a reprimand or a write-up for poor performance. Stephanie and Quinton from Goodwill never called me in to discuss a problem with guests or my performance.

I remember November 10, 2000, the day I got my five year award. The Marriott was proud of me, Goodwill was proud of me, and I was proud of what I had accomplished, of how far I had come from that man lying in the grass with a broken back or drunk and stoned in a strange apartment.

The hotel business changed after 9/11/2001. Business was so slow that hotels started laying off people, even folks who had been there 20 - 25 years. The Hotel told me they needed to thin down the day staff. They offered me the chance to work night shift with the Housekeeping Department. They told me if the night shift was too hard, they would try to get me back on days.

It was frustrating and hard for me to get to work at 10pm. It was hard for me to sit in the wheel chair from 10 at night until I got home the next morning. I wouldn't get home until around 8am, then I had to clean up, get in the bed and say my prayers. I couldn't sleep on that schedule. I would sleep for an hour, then I couldn't go back to sleep. I couldn't do the training and racing I wanted to. I couldn't go to church on Sunday the way I needed to. For three months I tried to work the night shift.

One morning they called me to Human Resources. The HR Director told me that due to continued low house count, they had to cut folks from the night housekeeping shift. I was disappointed. They didn't offer me the opportunity to return to day shift in any capacity. Later I learned that many other Goodwill folks had been terminated.

Several days later God opened another door for me. For the past several years I had been knowing the manager at the Decatur CVS Pharmacy. I told him my situation and he told me to come in the next day and start working.

My season at the Marriott was over.

Side Story by Henry Intili

I'm going to break into Ulysses' story to tell how his employment at the Marriott ended. This is a story that throws no credit on Marriott.

A few months after 9-11 when business was down, the Hotel Manager, RS, called a meeting in his office that I attended. He, The Hotel Lawyer, the Director of Human Resources and I (as the Nurse Practitioner for the Marriott Marquis) were there.

RS said he was concerned that guests were uncomfortable with disabled people in the public areas. He wanted them removed. You could have heard a pin drop. The lawyer cleared his throat and said that could be a legal problem. The Human Resources Manager (my manager) reminded RS that we had a contract with Goodwill and these folks had been good and effective employees. He wanted to know on what grounds they could be dismissed. I was more forceful and said removing these people is ethically and morally wrong. My manager backed me up.

RS was unmoved. He solved his problem by changing the daytime hours for the public area Goodwill employees to graveyard shift hours. Then he transferred them from public areas to housekeeping duties. Most of these people, including Ulysses, could not arrange for reliable third shift transportation. They either quit or where released due to failure to keep to a schedule.

Within a year the Goodwill program at the Marriott Marquis was closed. RS was promoted to a General Manager position at a new property. He asked me to join him at that property as the nurse practitioner. I politely declined.

I offered to support Ulysses in a federal lawsuit with ADA over the loss of his position. He declined.

STOMACH PROBLEMS

By 2007 my body was healthy, my mind was clear, and I had no issues with going home to visit and hang around with family, sons, daughters, grandchildren and friends. I wasn't having any problems traveling with my body or with stomach problems.

I took a greyhound bus on a Friday afternoon from Atlanta to Augusta. By 2007 even the busses had good accommodations for folks like me in a wheelchair. My family put me up in a hotel there. The next day they drove me to a town called Watley, Georgia where my sons and daughters are living. They checked me in to a hotel there.

It was a fine weekend, the best I had ever had with my family. Late Sunday afternoon I had a big dinner at the hotel and went to bed feeling good with myself and my body. Midnight I woke with a sense of having to use the bathroom. I swung out of the bed into my wheelchair and rolled to the bathroom where, using the handicapped bars, I was able to transfer to the toilet. When I returned to bed after cleaning myself, I slept for a while until I woke again with an incredible urge to use the bathroom.

During that night, from midnight to six am with only brief periods of sleep, I was back and forth from the bed to the bathroom. That morning I had a light breakfast at Huddle House and planned to spend the day at the school with my grandkids.

In the classroom with my grandkids I answered questions about my condition and showed the kids how to use the wheelchair. My stomach was fairly calm and I had a wonderful day with the children.

Back in the hotel on that Monday night, again my stomach had me back and forth to the bathroom. I wasn't in much pain, but I didn't understand why my stomach was acting up so much. Once again I had a difficult night with little sleep.

On Tuesday morning I ate a light breakfast at Huddle House and once more spent the day with the kids at school. By then I knew something was wrong. Something told me that I should pack my bags and return to Atlanta where I knew I could get the help I might need. Of course, that's not what I did. I kept pushing through the day.

Tuesday night was a repeat of Sunday and Monday. Up and down with little sleep. On Wednesday my oldest daughter came up to visit with me from Waynesboro. On the drive back to Waynesboro my daughter said she had to stop at WalMart. That was fine by me because by then I had to use the bathroom.

In the WalMart bathroom I saw blood in my stool. Now I was concerned and afraid. I didn't know what was going on with my body when I was having such a wonderful time with my children and grandchildren.

Back outside the store I called one of my doctors in Atlanta and explained to him what was happening. At that time I was working for CVS Pharmacy in Decatur (Atlanta). My doctor told me what I needed from the pharmacy and my daughter, now as concerned as I was, drove me to CVS for his prescriptions and some Depends.

My daughter's house, like so many places, was not wheelchair compatible. Especially not the bathroom. I had to struggle to move from my chair to the commode because the chair would not turn in the tight confines of her bathroom. It was fortunate that I bought the Depends because otherwise I would have made a messed myself bad.

I was deeply afraid that the medical problems from the 1990s that had kept me so long in the hospital had returned. It was so important to me to be with my family and grandkids that I hung in there with these problems longer than I should have.

Wednesday night at my daughter's house was a repeat of the earlier night at the hotel: Up to the bathroom many times with only brief periods of sleep in between. I was so afraid that my family would experience the smell of the constant diarrhea and messing myself.

After three days staying indoors at my daughter's house, I finally went to the hospital in Waynesboro. I was working for CVS then and had good insurance. At the hospital ER, first the admitting nurse and then the physician asked me a series of questions about my current painful symptoms, what I had eaten, and what were my usual bowel habits. They couldn't find anything wrong with me, gave me some general advice about stomach viruses and released me.

I told my daughter I was better and it was time for me to return to Atlanta. That was not the truth, but I was getting scared and didn't want to be a burden to her. I could only eat a little food. She arranged for me to get back to the hotel in Augusta where I started my visit. Once again for the next two nights – Friday and Saturday – I spent the night back and forth to the bathroom. My plan was to head back to Atlanta on Sunday morning.

Sunday morning I was so much worse that instead of getting on the bus for Atlanta, I had the hotel steward call an ambulance. They took me to Doctors' Hospital in Augusta. The ER physician, like the earlier doctor in Waynesboro, asked the same questions about what did I eat, what was my family history, and talked to me about stomach viruses "going around." They gave me ginger ale, soda crackers, a few medications, and prescriptions to fill in Atlanta.

I called my brother who came from Waynesboro and picked me up to drive me back to Atlanta. We made it back to Atlanta where I stopped at the CVS where I worked and filled the prescriptions from Augusta. My brother drove me home and stayed with me a few hours to make sure I was doing OK before he had to return to his home.

After he left, I called my pastor and asked the church to pray for me. I had another difficult night and could not go to work the next day. That Monday was another rough day and night. On Tuesday I woke weak and very frightened. I called an ambulance and they took me to Emory University Hospital in Decatur.

I spent the entire day at the hospital where they ran a series of tests to try to figure out what was happening to me, why I couldn't eat anything but a little fruit and crackers, why I was losing weight, and why I was constantly going to the bathroom. For several days they had me back and forth to the hospital while they ran tests on me.

During that week I accidentally cut my finger with some dirty glass. Now in addition to my bowel problem, I had serious infection problems with my right hand.

After a week the doctors came up with the idea that I had eaten corn or a similar grain that had somehow caused an infection in my intestines. They gave me the full names of everything, but I didn't write it down, didn't remember it afterwards, and still don't recall exactly what they said. (Why don't doctors write things down for you so you can remember what they say?).

A week later I started having problems with my left hand that a doctor said was gout. Now I was scared, very scared. My stomach, my right hand, my left hand – never had I experienced problems like this before. All this on top of being in a wheel chair. Simple things like taking fifteen minutes to get dressed now took an hour; getting out of a bath tub that used to take five minutes now took fifteen.

Emory sent me to Grady to have my right finger evaluated. The doctor there took one look and cut and drained the finger. They kept me in the hospital for two days to give me around the clock IV antibiotics. Now here I was taking antibiotics for my stomach, antibiotics for my finger, and pain medications for the gout. CVS called and told me that I hadn't been working for so long that my sick hours were almost out, and I was in danger of losing my health insurance.

I was so scared that every day I asked my church family to pray for me. Those folks called me and checked in on me. Every day I crawled out of my wheel chair, held on to the couch and prayed on my knees. I asked the Lord what was going on with my body. I was prepared to have the Lord take me, I was confident in my relationship with Jesus Christ. I was prepared to meet the Lord, but I wasn't ready, and I certainly wasn't eager.

My troubles with my stomach and hands slowly eased over the course of a full year. I returned to work at CVS on a reduced schedule that I slowly increased as my health returned.

In 2007 I learned what life was like for those folks much worse than me, for folks who didn't have the use of their hands and legs, for folks who were bed-bound, for folks who had to have others feed them and dress them, and for folks who had to depend on someone else for everything. Maybe I was in a wheelchair, maybe my legs didn't work anymore, but I had the strength to care for myself and live by myself.

From 2007 on my eyes were opened. God in his grace and his mercy, through my disability, showed me the way to him. I heard God speak to me on my knees and say that He needed me to pray for the families in hurricane Katrina, the folks in Columbine and Virginia Tech. He told me that those folks needed strength and hope the way I needed strength.

In 1990 when I fell from that balcony, God gave me the opportunity to get my life right. In 2007, again he gave me an opportunity to get closer to Him and His ways.

During that awful year I continued to wheel myself everywhere. Some folks wanted me to change to an electric wheel chair. I never permitted that. I continued to push myself around my house, up and down the ramp into my house, down the street, into my church and everything else. I had to stay strong, I had to stay focused.

A year after my troubles started, I returned to my racing bike and lifting weights. I couldn't put too much pressure on my stomach and hands, but I was determined to return to my chosen sport. By July, 2008 I was able to do the Peachtree Road Race again.

By December I was back in the CVS stockroom preparing for Christmas. One day I turned quickly and a stock shelf collapsed and hit me on the back of the neck. I didn't think much about it until the next morning when I could barely turn my head and my while upper body was stiff. My manager made me report the incident to Workers Compensation. Once again I was out of work for several months. As much as I wanted to return to work, the Workers Compensation physician would not let me return until I was completely better.

PROBLEMS WITH SOCIAL SECURITY

By 2009 everything was doing well. I was going back to church, back to racing, training, back to work as much as I could at CVS. Then here comes Social Security giving me a hard time.

They sent me a letter saying they were going to cut my benefits off. There is no way to tell you how important those SS benefits were and are to me. I wasn't making enough money with my part-time work at CVS to pay for my small place, food, medicine, special medical goods, and everything else I needed to live a minimal lifestyle.

Social Security said that I owed them over $100,000. How could that be?

They said I made too much money when I was at the Marriott, saying I was making too much money now, saying they were going to cut off my benefits, saying I owed them over $100,000 back. One hundred thousand dollars! I don't believe I even made $100,000 in my years at Marriott and CVS. I wasn't drinking, I wasn't smoking, I wasn't doing drugs, I wasn't chasing women, I didn't own a car – I was living on the edge with no spare cash, and these people thought I had $100,000 in extra income!

For weeks I had to go to downtown Atlanta to talk to the SS office. Sometimes twice a week. My pastor came with me, Sally Atwell from Shepherd Spinal Center came with me. One time Sally prepared an entire folder of paperwork from Shepherd. The lady at Social Security didn't even look at the paperwork. She said: *This paperwork has nothing to do with your case.* She pushed it to the side with disrespect for me and Shepherd and continued to berate me for stealing money from the government. She looked me square in the eye with a straight face and said: *You go over one penny what you're supposed to make and we are going to cut you off.*

Here I am a man in a wheelchair with a part-time job stocking shelves at a pharmacy, trying my best to work, never claiming total disability – and the government people saying I owed them more money than I have ever made in my whole life, and this hard-hearted woman saying she was going to cut off all my benefits which would throw me out on the street. I was already living on the edge.

I didn't know what to do. I had never been in this kind of situation before in my life. With the help of my church and Sally, and the grace of God, they did not cut off my check. I know folks that year who did lose their checks. Why was the government taking money away from cripple people?

Throughout 2010 they made me go to the downtown Atlanta SS office to pick up my check in person. Usually I had to wait two hours for them to sign the check and release it to me. They would not mail my check to me.

Many times Sally came down to the SS Office with me. Many times she met with the manager there. They kept losing the paperwork that Shepherd sent, they denied ever receiving paperwork from me.

The Social Security lady wanted to take $350 a month from my paycheck to pay back the $100,000 they said I owed. We told her that would leave me with no money for food or medicine or Depends. She didn't care. She had not the slightest sympathy for me or my situation. All she wanted to discuss was the money she said I owed the government.

Finally Sally and my pastor argued her and her manager down to $250 and then $150 a month. The government must be in terrible need of money to take $1800 a year from a man in a wheelchair making minimum wage who wants to be a productive member of society. With all the cheating and fraud in the system, to vindictively go after a cripple who's trying to work is something I cannot understand.

I had to reduce my hours at CVS to two days a week to stay below the minimum income the Social Security folks demanded. When I went part-time at CVS, I lost my health insurance and dental plan and my other benefits with CVS. That drop in income plus the money I had to pay the government every month severely cut into what I could do for my health and my living.

I fell behind in my light bill, the rent, and the water bill. I paid what I could every month, but I was falling behind worse and worse. The people in my church and friends came to my aid and I thank God for them. The travelling expenses for my racing dried up and again I had to depend on the help of others. But I never lost sight of Psalm 121: *I lifted my eyes unto the hills whence cometh my help. My help cometh from the Lord.* I meditated on the Psalm from morning to night.

I was living under Section 8 housing at that time. My landlord told me I had to pay him the rent. But six months later I learned that he was being paid by Section 8. At that point someone owed me $2200. The landlord said he wasn't going to pay me. And Social Security didn't want to pay me and go after the landlord for the money. With my pastor's help, we arranged a meeting at the church with Social Security so I could have witnesses to any agreement. After a year of fighting with these awful people from the government, I needed all the help I could get, even if bringing God and God's house into the mix was needed.

They finally agreed to pay me a small amount of money every month against the money I had paid to the landlord.

All this mess with the government in 2010 and 2011left me angry, upset and confused. I tried to put these feeling away, to not show my feelings to these government people or even to my friends. These were negative feelings that could drag me down, that could affect my focus for training and racing. It's hard to push the training when you're down and discouraged. I could have started back to drinking or smoking or taking the drugs or laying around the house and being sorry for myself. God and Psalm 121 got me through those hard times. I heard a voice inside me saying: *Don't give up.*

I tell you I shed a few tears now and then because things weren't going right. But I never felt sorry for myself. Many times I went to my pastor and told him my troubles. He eased my mind and put my problems in God's hands.

I'm not putting my pastor on a padded stool. He helped me and encouraged me. Whenever he told me something was going to happen, eventually it did. On days when I knew I had to go to the government office and wait hours for them to see me, he told me to stay calm and show them respect – they owed me the money and they would finally deliver it to me.

By 2012 my problems with the government seemed to be resolved. I had to live from paycheck to paycheck. Between my income from the job and the government support, I had too much income to qualify for food stamps and other assistance programs. I would have been better off financially and in my living conditions if I didn't work and try to be somebody!

That year I really wanted to go home and spend time with family, but there wasn't enough money.

In order to enter a race, there had to be money for entrance fees, money for transportation and food, money to make sure the tires and bike and gloves were in good repair, money for a hotel room, and money for any of a dozen other things that would always go wrong.

Through 2012 I was able to go to a few races. God let me win some prize money, and that really helped. I always remembered to pay my tithes. When your income is limited like mine was, sometimes it's hard to pay your tithes to the blessings of the Kingdom of God. I always remembered that there are people out there worse than I am, people who don't have nothing.

2014 was a very difficult year. Things had not worked out this year the way I planned. I wanted to do the Chicago Marathon and the funds were not in place for me to do that. I wanted to do the Japan Marathon in November and the funds were not in place for that. Maybe I'm in a place now where I really need to trust in the Lord and not look to friends, church and family.

The government didn't want me to earn any more income than what I can make working one day a week. That's not enough money for me to live and go to these races on my own. I accept God's blessings for what he's given me, but I found myself on a very hard budget last year. Sometimes I had no choice – I had to turn to family and friends for help to pay my bills and keep enough food in the house. I thank them even though that's not where my heart is, to ask them for my needs.

I thank the Lord that he has stayed with me for my spiritual needs, to stay prayed up, to stay studying His Word. His help lets me stay surrounded by positive people and not negative people talking negative all the time. I hear negative talk on my job, when I'm riding the train, when I'm on the Marta bus, and when I'm out in the community. I know I can't focus on the negative stuff of living. I ask the Holy Spirit to help me focus my life on the positive. When you focus on the negative, you become confused and discouraged; you lay around the house doing nothing. Then the Devil comes and really beats you up.

Sometimes this year, when I'm really down, I think God has forgotten about me. I know he hasn't because he said *He will never leave me, He will never forsake me*. Friends can leave you sometime, family can turn their backs on you sometime, even the church can turn their back on you. That don't mean these people don't love you. It means they want you to try to meet your own needs and to look to the Lord, and not to depend completely on them.

I force myself to stay positive. Every week I go to the local elementary school, Norwood, to hang out with the kids and encourage them to be all they can.

Nancy from Grady calls me to help her with spinal injury patients. I know how discouraging spinal injuries can be, I know the anger you feel when your body can't do what you want. God calls to me to encourage these people. I put on my best face so they see me positive and not discouraged about my injuries.

For the past several weeks I've been training whenever I can at a local Kroger Plaza. There's a mile course I race at that plaza. I see young men and women standing around digging in the garbage can, begging for a dollar to get something to eat or to buy something in the package store. When I see that I know how blessed I am. That could be me in a corner seated in a wheelchair with my hand out aggravating people to give them fifty cents or begging for money. Maybe they don't even have a place to stay.

I could be in that place, I know where that place is. But I'm not in that place. Even when I find myself complaining, even when I find myself wanting to give up, even when I find myself discouraged, even when I find myself setting around the house and not doing a thing, I don't let the negative take over me. I have a place to live, I have food, I have lights, I'm able enough to bathe myself, I can put on clean clothes.

Last week a woman chased me down when I took a short break from racing around the plaza. "I recognized your face from working at CVS. Is your name Ulysses Elijah? I met you several years ago. You told me your story, how you were an evil man and what happened to change you. I want you to know how you inspired me when I was in a bad way. You were a blessing in my life. Now I'm a school teacher. I want to take your picture and tell your story to the children in my classroom."

The other day when I was working at CVS, a young girl came into the store with her mama. That girl looked real hard at me. She tugged at her mother's arm and asked her: "Mama, why is that man in a wheelchair?"

I wheeled over to that little girl and told her: "I was on drugs. I got myself in trouble. I wouldn't listen to anyone. That's how I ended up in this chair." That girl listened to me. I knew she understood. "I didn't listen to my teachers or my family. I dropped out of school. I stole and lied to get my drugs. I didn't do what God asked me to." I gave a card to my website to the girl's mama.

These are the things that encourage me in my life.

PEACH TREE ROAD RACE 2014.

By 2014, the Wheelchair Division had added a new category: Grand Masters. This group was for racers over 50 years old. There were five of us who qualified for this. I had been racing for 20 years in the Peachtree and had never won.

Rocky West, a powerful man in a chair and like me over 50, had beaten me year after year. This year I was determined to race past him. He's also on the Shepherd Team and, like me, he trains hard there several times a week. Rocky has beaten me consistently, especially during some years when I was slacking.

Laura and Nancy had me at the starting line by 6am so I could warm up on this beautiful, humid Atlanta morning. I ate light – a granola bar and half a banana.

I drank water through the night and before the race. There is no place to carry water on your wheelchair, and no way to break your arm rhythm to take a drink. People along the 10K route offer you water in bottles and cups. But no wheelchair racer that wants to win is going to stop for a drink. You push through your thirst.

In 2014 the Race had five groups: Open Men (20-40), Open Women, Masters (40-50), Grand Masters (50+) and Quads. They start in that order with one minute between starts. When I started passing racers from groups in front of me, I knew it was going to be a good race.

With only five people in our Grand Masters group, we all started in one line. I nodded at Rocky, who nodded back. They dropped the flag and I raced ahead of Rocky, spinning my wheels as hard and fast as I ever had.

He passed me on the first downhill. Rocky is heavier that I am and knows how to use his weight to gain speed downhill.

This year I had a plan. I had been training extra hard on hills, going up hills rather than training on flat areas. When we started the famous Heartbreak Hill near Shepherd Center, we were close to each other with Rocky in the lead. That's when I turned on the juice and powered past him with all my extra training. In the July heat with that effort, the sweat was pouring off me, but I was determined to beat him this year.

Half way up the hill I zipped past Rocky and never looked back. The race was mine. I blessed God with all my heart when I soared through the finish line with my arms in the air. 30 minutes! That's 4 minutes faster than my first race 20 years earlier.

I slow-wheeled to the Shepherd area, got lots of high-fives and hugs, and grabbed a tee-shirt that every participant gets. Changed over to my regular chair and downed bottles of ice water.

I was about to leave when Matt Eaton from Shepherd stopped me. "Ulysses, where are you going? You can't leave. Come with me. You won!"

I went up on the main stage with the other winners and wheeled to the front. In the bright sunshine under that Georgia blue sky, they gave me a trophy and took pictures. Lots of applause from the people out front stirred my soul.

My thoughts: *Thank you, Jesus! I like this. I want it again!*

FINAL THOUGHTS.

I know that I am not in this race of life by myself. Thirty years ago I was all messed up and confused. Jesus said he would never leave me or forsake me, and I am so grateful that he shared his grace with me.

As I close my story, I pray that these words will be a blessing to you and your family and anyone who reads this book.

Ulysses Elijah

END NOTES by Henry Intili

I met Ulysses when I took the position of Associate Health Nurse at the Marriott Marquis Hotel in 1997. I live in awe of his strength, fortitude and faith. I have told his story a hundred times to anyone who will listen.

Ulysses and I have a special, personal bond. We both have our birthday on November 11. We were both born when 11-11 was Armistice Day, not Veterans Day. Every year we try to get together for dinner on November 11. My wife and I can think of no better way to celebrate my birthday than in the company of someone we admire and look up to.

It has been my pleasure to help Ulysses with the story of his odyssey. The original Ulysses of ancient Greece would be proud.

Other Books by Henry Intili

Travel Junkies (Backpack and Canoe)

Travel Junkies 2 (Backpack and Canoe 2)

Travel Junkies 3

eTravel Books (Available on amazon.com and henryintili.com)

New York City Days (Young and Single in New York City)

Farm Days (Hippie Years)

The Trigamist

Anello and the Garibaldi Reunion

Anello and the Soldiers of WW II

Poems, Ghost Stories and Palm Readers

Three Plays (Good Evening Gloria's, Farm Days, and Yvonne)

Two One Act Plays

Under the Nurse's Cap

The Weenie Clinic

The I.M.P. Affair

The Adventures of Tony and Woof

Further Adventures of Tony and Woof

Recipes From Gloria's Restaurant

More Recipes From Gloria's Restaurant

E-Books by Henry available at Amazon.com and www.henryintili.com:

A Walk on the Dingle Way, Ireland

Canoe the Noatak River, Gates of the Arctic NP, Alaska

A Walk through Tuscany, from Florence to Siena, Italy

A Canoe Trip on the Missouri River, 100 Miles in Montana

A Hike in Iceland on the Thorsborne Trail

A Hike in Needles, Canyonlands National Monument, Utah

Hike the Brazeau River Trail, Jasper National Park, Canada

A Hike in the Canadian Rockies, The White Goat Wilderness

A Bicycle Trip in Holland, Leiden to Haarlem.

Explore Alaska by Canoe and a Rent-A-Wreck Van

Ghosts, Spirits and Palm Readers.

Anello and the Garibaldi Reunion in Sicily

Anello and the Soldiers Returned From WW II

Exploring, Hiking and Biking in New Zealand